several heights. This creates a pleasing arrangement and fills the space nicely. Again, work in odd numbers. If I'm making an arrangement with 5 candles, I will use candles in 3 different heights. Sometimes you can fake the different heights by placing some of the candles on wood blocks which you camouflage with decorative elements.

Shape. Don't limit yourself to traditional pillar candles. You can find round, square, and oval candles... tall, short, fat and skinny candles. Experiment with combining candles of different shapes and sizes in your arrangements.

Color. Just about anything goes when it comes to choosing colors for your candlescaping projects. I often use 3 or 4 different colors in one arrangement. On the other hand, I also love the simplicity of several ivory candles grouped together. You'll want to coordinate your candle colors with the flowers, ribbon or other embellishments.

Candle Burning Tips

Why didn't someone tell us this stuff sooner?

Burning Time. To insure the life of pillar candles, burn them each time for at least one hour for every inch of candle width. This allows the wax to melt to the outside edge of the candle and prevents a tunnel from burning down the center. For example, burn a 3" diameter candle for 3 hours. For multiple wick candles, divide the number of hours by the number of wicks. For example, if you have a 6" triple wick candle, you will want to burn it for at least 2 hours at a time.

Trim Wicks. Each time you burn a candle, trim the wick to ¼". This prevents smoking and keeps the wick from turning over into the melting wax.

Protect Table Tops. Always place candles on or in a heat resistant container to protect counters and furniture. Many votive candles liquefy as they burn. Always place votive candles in a holder large enough to hold the melted wax.

Safety First. Never leave a burning candle unattended. Be aware of the items you put in a candle arrangement. Make sure that flammable materials cannot fall into the flames.

Now the real fun begins! You can use just about anything for your candlescaping project, as long as you use common sense and good judgement. For example, if you place candle holders inside a wicker basket, you can use it for a candlescape. I like to use teacups, clay pots, wicker baskets, and household items.

Choosing Embellishments

Here are just a few ideas to get you started:

Flowers. You can create a beautiful candlescape by placing flowers around the base of your candles. Look for mixed floral bushes, which often feature flowers in several sizes and colors.

Ribbon. Turn a candle from plain to pretty with the simple addition of ribbon. Tie ribbon around a candle grouping finishing with a nice bow. Or you might try placing a bow nestled in among the flowers at the base of the candle arrangement. Experiment with different types of ribbon, from sheers to raffia, metallics to fabric, thin styles to wide styles.

Naturals. Sometimes the most simple objects create the most beautiful candlescape. Try polished rocks, moss or potpourri arranged at the base of a candle or group of candles. It is also fun to experiment with seeds, seashells, nuts and dried flowers. If you're working with floating candles, don't forget to try fresh flowers and fruit!

Collections. Antique buttons, seashells from your vacation or glass ornaments from your mother's collection… most of us have objects with special meanings. Try using these items in your candle arrangements. On the other hand, don't be afraid to be whimsical! Candles nestled in candy corn make for a festive Halloween decoration. Don't forget a strategically placed spider to properly spook your guests!

A.

B.

C.

D.

Choosing a Base

It is extremely important to place candle arrangements on heat resistant surfaces. You can accomplish this in several ways.

A. Individual Candle Holders. You can purchase glass candle holders at a local craft store. These are simple glass jars or plates made to hold candles as well as catch any dripping wax. If you're making a candlescape for a large area such as a dining table, you may wish to place the candles in individual holders on the table. Then build the arrangement around the candle holders. Since you won't be able to move the arrangement in one piece, this technique is best for a permanent candlescape.

B. Candle Plates. There are many types of plates and trays designed specifically for candle arrangements. However, don't limit yourself to candle pieces, you can use charger plates, trays, mirrors, serving pieces, wicker baskets and many other found objects.

C. Floating Candle Dishes. You can purchase garden dishes and glass bowls designed specifically for floating candles. Once again, you don't have to be limited to traditional pieces. You can use crystal bowls, glasses, teacups or any heat resistant container that holds water.

D. Other Containers. Many of the bases and holders used in this book were found in the designer's home. Everything else was purchased at a local craft store.

Starting Simple

Some of my favorite candle arrangements are the most simple! Take a candle from simple to spectacular with the addition of a few simple elements.

MATERIALS:
• Light Green 3-wick pillar candle
• Clear glass triangle plate
• Green and White sea glass

INSTRUCTIONS:
Place candle on plate. Add sea glass to cover bottom of dish and base of candle.

1. Choose a base.

2. Choose a candle.

3. Add the embellishments.

Designer's Tip

Notice how the same technique can create very different looks. If you like the 'feel' of an arrangement, don't be afraid to adapt it to match your home's decor. Change the color, size, or style of the elements to suit your decorating needs.

Starting Simple

It is easy as 1-2-3.

- Choose your base
- Choose your candle
- Add embellishments

You can change the look of your favorite candle and candle holder by simply changing the embellishments!

- Glass Marbles & Nuggets
- Seashells
- Acrylic Ice Cubes
- Sea Glass

Marbles & Nuggets

Seashells

Acrylic Ice Cubes

Sea Glass

Simple Celestial

When I saw this star plate, I just knew I had to use it as a candle holder! A unique textured candle surrounded by ice cubes makes a simple statement.

MATERIALS:
• Silver star plate
• Lavender pillar candle
• Acrylic ice cubes
INSTRUCTIONS:
Place candle in plate. Arrange ice cubes as desired.

Designer's Tip

Notice how the same technique can create very different looks. If you like the 'feel' of an arrangement, don't be afraid to adapt it to match your home's decor. Change the color, size, or style of the elements to suit your decorating needs.

Simple Zen

An elegant, square plate inspired a simple candlescape. Natural polished stones and a rustic candle give this arrangement a calming quality.

MATERIALS:
• Oriental plate
• Square natural pillar candle
• Polished stones
INSTRUCTIONS:
Place candle in center of plate. Add stones around base of candle.

Simple Chinese Characters

Candles with special sentiments in Chinese characters make a serene candlescape.

MATERIALS:
- 7" White triangle candle
- 4" White pillar candle
- 11" White dinner plate
- White sand
- Black polished stones
- Bamboo sticks
- Chinese character rubber stamps
- Stamp pad
- Black paint pen

INSTRUCTIONS:
Stamp characters on candles, let dry. Paint with pen. Arrange candles in plate. Add stones and bamboo sticks.

Down by the Sea

Everyone loves a day at the seashore. Remember fresh ocean breezes and the warm sandy beaches with candlescapes. Use the seashell treasures you collected to make these arrangements even more special.

MATERIALS:
• 16" terra cotta saucer
• 5 pillar candles in different heights, colors and shapes
• 2 Votive candles and holders
• Sand
• Seashells
• Air plants

INSTRUCTIONS:
Arrange the candles as desired. Pour sand into the tray around the candles. Arrange seashells on top of the sand, making sure some of the sand remains visible. Place air plants as desired.

Rocky Shore

You can almost hear the ebb and flow of the tide on a rocky coastline when this candle arrangement graces your table.

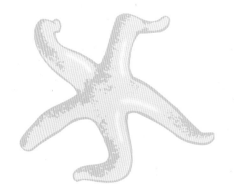

MATERIALS:
- 3 Ivory pillar candles in different sizes
- Two 2¼" terra cotta pots
- 4" and 14" terra cotta saucers
- Rocks
- Assorted seashells

INSTRUCTIONS:
Place candles in pots. Arrange pots in saucer. Fill saucer with enough rocks to secure pots. Add seashells.

Seashore

This candlescape is reminiscent of a walk along the seashore when damp stones and seashells catch the rays of the setting sun.

MATERIALS:
• Large and small Ivory mini pillar candles
• 12" Clear glass plate
• Polished stones
• Assorted seashells

INSTRUCTIONS:
Place candles on plate. Add stones to secure candles. Arrange seashells as desired.

Designer's Tip

If you wish to use votive candles in your candlescape, make sure they are in glass or ceramic holders. Many votive candles liquefy as they burn.

Candle & Seashells

What a lovely way to display those treasured seashells you collected on last year's vacation at the beach.

MATERIALS:
• 4" pillar candle
• 7" brandy snifter
• Assorted seashells
• Natural raffia

INSTRUCTIONS:
Place candle in bottom of brandy snifter. Fill around candle with seashells as shown. Tie raffia bow.

Shell Candle

Use a large, perfect seashell for a casual candleholder.

MATERIALS:
• Scallop floating candle
• White sand
• 7" scallop shell and assorted small seashells

INSTRUCTIONS:
Pour sand in shell to desired depth. Push candle into sand. Arrange seashells.

1. Place marbles in the bowl.

2. Fill bowl with water and add floating candles.

3. Sprinkle confetti on water.

Valentine Romance

Set the mood for your romantic Valentine's Day celebration with this floating candle centerpiece.

MATERIALS:
• 9" garden dish
• 3 Red and 2 White heart floating candles
• White and Red marbles
• Heart confetti

INSTRUCTIONS: Gently place marbles in bottom of garden dish. Fill with water and place floating candles. Sprinkle confetti over the surface of the water and on the table around the bowl.

Hearts & Flowers

Say 'I Love You' with a sentimental hearts and flowers candlescape.

MATERIALS:
- 5¼" Clear ivy bowl
- Red heart and rose floating candles
- One yard of 1½" sheer Red wire edge ribbon
- Red food coloring

INSTRUCTIONS:
Fill bowl with water and add food coloring. Float candle and tie bow around bowl.

Fruit Bowl

Make this quick and easy centerpiece for your summer entertaining.

MATERIALS:
• Floating candle bowl
• 6 mini floating candles
• Lemons
• Oranges
• Kumquats
• Cranberries
• Daisy blossoms

INSTRUCTIONS:
Fill candle bowl with water and place floaters inside. Thinly slice lemons and oranges. Cut some of the slices in half and quarters. Place citrus slices, cranberries, kumquats and daisy blossoms on surface of water.

Apple Bowl

Instead of an apple bob, float apple candles in a bowl for your autumn parties.

MATERIALS:
• Floating candle bowl
• 7 apple shape floating candles

INSTRUCTIONS:
Fill candle bowl with water and place floaters inside.

Cranberry Christmas

Set a simply sophisticated holiday table with this classic arrangement as a centerpiece.

MATERIALS:
• Candle bowl
• 7 mini Ivory floating candles
• Fresh cranberries

INSTRUCTIONS:
Fill the bowl with water and float candles on top. Sort through cranberries and remove any blemished or soft berries. Gently float cranberries on the water completely covering the surface. Coax candles into place if needed.

Designer's Tip

Make each guest at your holiday celebration feel extra-special. A single floating candle in a votive cup makes the perfect complement to this Cranberry Christmas centerpiece. Simply float a candle in a large votive cup and surround with cranberries.

Tea Party

You don't have to be a tea lover to fall in love with this idea! It's the perfect way to decorate for a bridal shower, luncheon… and of course an elegant tea party!

MATERIALS:
• Teacups
• Teapot
• Tea lights
• Fresh flowers

INSTRUCTIONS

Arrange fresh flowers in teapot. Place tea lights inside the teacups and arrange around the teapot. It doesn't get much easier than this!

Romance in Bloom

Simple painted flowers and candles in matching colors make a delicate arrangement for a ladies' luncheon.

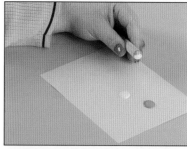

1. Dip paintbrush handle in White and Pink or Purple.

2. Swirl colors together with stylus or paintbrush handle.

3. Add dot flowers and leaves.

MATERIALS:
- 8" glass plate
- Delta PermEnamel Paint (Surface Cleaner and Conditioner, Tropical Purple, White Frost, White, Sea Foam Green, Desert Blush Pink, Crocus Yellow, Clear Gloss Glaze)
- Foam brush
- #8 flat brush
- ¾" wash brush
- Stylus
- 3 pillar candles in different shapes, colors and sizes

INSTRUCTIONS:
Read instructions on Perm Enamel bottle and follow them carefully. Wash plate thoroughly with soap and water and dry. Brush Surface Cleaner and Conditioner on the back of the plate and allow to dry about 20 minutes. Use foam brush to apply White Frost to the back of the plate. The paint will appear streaky but will even out as it dries. Allow to dry and apply a second coat of White Frost. When the back of the plate is completely dry, apply Clear Gloss Glaze. Allow the back of the plate to dry completely before painting the front. Brush Surface Cleaner and Conditioner on the rim of the plate and allow to dry about 20 minutes. The flowers are made with the handle of the foam brush. Dip one half of the handle into White, the other half into Tropical Purple or Desert Blush Pink. Touch the handle onto the surface of the plate and lift. Use the stylus to swirl the colors together. Repeat to create clusters of flowers around the rim of the plate. Add Sea Foam Green leaves. Baby's breath is made by dipping the stylus into paint and applying dots on the glass. Do not add more paint, the dots will get smaller as the paint is applied. When the paint is completely dry, use ¾" wash brush to apply Clear Gloss Glaze to the rim of the plate. Place candles on plate.

Winter Elegance

Rich blue candles and delicate white blossoms on a silver tray will add elegance to winter entertaining decor.

MATERIALS:
- 14" Silver Plate
- 5 Dark Blue candles in different heights and shapes
- White and Blue artificial hydrangea blooms

INSTRUCTIONS:
Arrange the candles as desired on the plate. Snip or pull individual petals from the hydrangea blooms. Sprinkle the flowers around the candle being sure to fill all empty spaces.

1. Arrange the candles on a plate.

2. Remove flowers from stem.

3. Fill spaces between candles with flowers.

Designer's Tip

When arranging your candles, keep in mind how the viewer will see your candlescape. If it will be a centerpiece, you will need to make sure the arrangement is pleasing from all angles. Most often your candlescape will be seen from one direction only, so you will not need to worry about what the back looks like.

Natural Charm

This simple arrangement of candles is softened with the scent of potpourri and a sheer bow.

MATERIALS:
• Bamboo tray
• Potpourri
• 4 Pillar candles in different heights and shapes
• Taper candle and holder
• 2 yards of floral ribbon
INSTRUCTIONS:
Arrange the candles as desired. Arrange potpourri around the candles being careful not to let any fall into the votive cups. Tie a bow and add to the edge of the tray.

Patio Party Lights

Cast a warm glow over guests at your next summer party with a cluster of clay pot lanterns. A small pot bearing each guest's name adds an elegant touch to a casual affair.

1. Paint inside of pots Glorious Gold.

2. Write names on parchment paper.

3. Attach names to pots and insert candles.

Patio Party Lights

MATERIALS:
- Assorted sizes of terra cotta pots
- Pillar candles and tea lights
- DecoArt Dazzling Metallics Glorious Gold acrylic paint
- Foam brush
- Parchment paper
- Black fine-tipped marker
- Double stick tape

INSTRUCTIONS:

Paint the inside of the clay pots Glorious Gold and allow to dry thoroughly. Arrange pots on the center of your table and place candles inside. Make sure candles are shorter than the pots otherwise that cool summer breeze will blow out candles!

Use a permanent marker to write each guest's name on a piece of parchment paper. Attach to a 3" clay pot with double stick tape. Insert a tea light in each pot and place at the appropriate place setting. These lanterns are sure to bring a smile to everyone's face!

Bamboo Pair

Simple and natural… make a Feng Shui statement with bamboo candleholders.

MATERIALS:
- 3" pillar and large votive candles
- 3" x 6" and 3" x 3" Clear glass cylinders
- 2 bamboo placemats
- Jute twine

INSTRUCTIONS:

Wrap a placemat around each cylinder and remove excess bamboo. Trim height. Tie ends together with weaving thread. Wrap twine around cylinders referring to photo. Insert candles.

Southwest Glow

Bright Southwest colors enliven these unusual candle covers.

MATERIALS:
- Assorted 4" terra cotta pots
- 2" terra cotta pot
- One 4" and seven 5" terra cotta saucers
- Acrylic paint (Green, Orange, Hot Pink, Purple, Light Green, Yellow, Pink and Fuchsia)
- Southwest themed rubber stamps
- Black ink stamp pad
- Tea lights
- Foam brush
- Acrylic spray sealer
- Drill and 1/8" masonry bit

INSTRUCTIONS:

Drill holes in one side of each pot. Paint pots and saucers referring to photo. Stamp design. Spray with sealer. Arrange pots, saucers and candles as desired.

Patio Party Lanterns

As dusk settled over a party one summer after-noon, my friend Julie brought out these charming lanterns to light the tables and patio. Your guests are sure to be just as delighted as I was.

MATERIALS:
- Glass canning jars in various sizes
- Pillar candles in various sizes
- Black craft wire
- Sand

INSTRUCTIONS:

Cut a one yard long piece of craft wire. Wrap it around the rim of the jar and twist to secure leaving the ends long. Twist the 2 pieces of wire together making one thicker wire. Form a handle by securing the ends of the wire to the opposite side of the jar. Trim any remaining wire. Now you can easily transport the lanterns during your party!

Pour about 2 inches of sand into each jar. Place a small pillar candle in the sand, pushing down until it is secure.

Patio Aglow

Keep the bugs away from your patio party in style with this blooming candleholder and citronella candle.

1. Twist wire around top of canning jar.

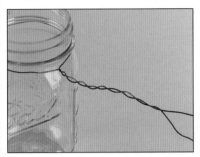

2. Twist ends together to form one wire.

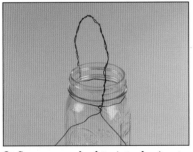

3. Secure end of twisted wire to other side of jar.

4. Add sand and insert candle.

Designer's Tip

For outdoor decorating, purchase citronella candles to keep insects away. You can find them in just about any shape and size including pillars, tea lights and votives.

MATERIALS:
- 8" terra cotta pot and saucer
- 5½" terra cotta bowl with citronella candle
- Green acrylic paint
- Multicolor raffia
- Assorted pot rim hangers.
- Foam brush
- Acrylic spray sealer
- Potting soil
- Blooming plants

INSTRUCTIONS:

Paint pot Green and spray with sealer. Fill pot with soil, arrange plants around edge. Place a candle in a pot in the center. Tie raffia around pot. Place hangers on pot rims.

Tradition of the Advent Wreath

For centuries, the Christian church has set aside the four weeks prior to Christmas as the season of Advent - a time to prepare for the holiday and the second coming of Christ. The advent wreath is traditionally a circle of evergreens with five candles. The circle symbolizes the wholeness of God with the greenery representing eternal life. Traditionally, the color lit on the first two Sundays of advent is purple or lavender which symbolizes hope and peace. The pink third candle represents joy and the fourth purple candle symbolizes love. The center candle is symbolic of Christ and is always white. The Christ candle is lit on Christmas Eve or Christmas Day. The lighting of the candles is a time when families are encouraged to read a passage of scripture, sing a hymn and pray together.

1. Place candle holder in wreath and fluff greenery.

2. Remove blooms from bush and insert in wreath.

3. Tie bows and insert in wreath.

Advent Wreath

The lighting of Advent candles is a seasonal tradition for many families.

MATERIALS:
- Advent candle ring
- Advent candles (3 Purple and one Pink taper or 4 tapers of same color)
- White pillar candle
- 24" pine wreath
- 12 yards of sheer floral ribbon
- 4 poinsettia picks
- Floral wire
- Glue gun and glue sticks

INSTRUCTIONS:
Place advent candle holder on wreath. Fluff wreath so that the candle holder and wreath become one. Secure with floral wire. Make 4 sheer ribbon bows. Attach one bow to the right of each candle holder. Place poinsettia picks between the candle holders. Place the advent taper candles in the candle holder and the white pillar in the center of the wreath.

Christmas Floaters

Set a breathtaking holiday table with floating candles and florals.

MATERIALS:
- 14", 11¾" and 8½" glass cylinders
- 2 large votive bowls
- Dark Red, Frosted Green and Clear marbles
- 3" Ivory, Burgundy and Sage floating candles
- Ivory, Burgundy and Sage mini floating candles
- 12" x 18" mirror
- Poinsettia bush
- Greenery picks
- Wire cutters

INSTRUCTIONS:
Carefully wipe any fingerprints or dust from glass candle holders. Gently place marbles in the bottom of each container using a single color for each. Fill with water and arrange on mirror. Place one floating candle in each container making sure the candle and marble colors contrast. Use wire cutters to cut poinsettia blooms from bush. Arrange the blooms around the candle holders on the mirror. Add greenery picks.

1. Place marbles in containers.

2. Fill with water, add candles and arrange on mirror.

3. Arrange flowers on mirror between containers.

4. Add greenery picks.

Christmas Pedestal

a Raise your Christmas centerpiece to new heights of elegance with this pedestal arrangement of poinsettias, greenery, grapes and a bright red candle.

MATERIALS:
- Pedestal base
- Triple wick candle
- 3 greenery sprays
- 4 poinsettia blooms
- 3 berry picks
- 2 grape clusters
- Spanish moss
- Floral foam
- Floral wire
- Wire cutters
- Glue gun and glue sticks

INSTRUCTIONS:
Place triple wick candle in center of pedestal bowl. Cut floral foam into thin pieces and place in bowl around candle. Foam should surround the candle snugly. Secure with hot glue. Cover foam with a thin layer of Spanish moss. Bend 5" pieces of floral wire into U shapes to secure the moss to the foam. Hot glue is difficult to use with moss! Cut greenery into small clusters. Insert into foam creating an elongated base for your arrangement. Refer to photo for placement. Place grape clusters on either side of the candle. Cut berry picks into several clusters of stems and insert around the greenery. Place poinsettia blooms around the candle.

1. Place foam around base of candle.

2. Cover foam with moss.

3. Insert greenery clusters.

4. Add berry picks and grapes.

5. Place flowers around candle.

Cinnamon Christmas

A glowing candle and the scent of cinnamon… what more do you need to bring the spirit of Christmas home?

MATERIALS:
- 6" x 5" White 4 wick candle
- Cinnamon sticks
- 2 poinsettia blossoms
- 3 yards each of Red and Gold 1½" sheer wire edge ribbon
- Hot glue gun and glue

INSTRUCTIONS:
Glue cinnamon sticks to candle. Cut ribbons in half, wrap around candle and tie bows. Glue poinsettias on bows.

Holiday Pedestal

A pre-made greenery centerpiece is the starting point for this beautiful floral design.

MATERIALS:
- Greenery centerpiece
- 6 yards of ribbon
- 4 poinsettia blooms
- 6 hydrangea blooms
- 2 berry picks
- 4 pillar candles in different heights and shapes
- 1 ball candle
- Floral wire
- Wire cutters
- Glue gun and glue sticks

INSTRUCTIONS:
Make 2 bows with the floral ribbon. Attach one bow on each side of the candle plate. Secure with floral wire. Cut poinsettia blooms from stems and add to greenery base keeping them near the center of the arrangement. Refer to photo for placement. Secure with hot glue. Place one hydrangea bloom near the end of each side of the greenery. Add remaining hydrangea blooms among the greenery. Cut berry picks into several clusters of stems and add them around the poinsettia and hydrangea blooms. Arrange candles on plate, light and enjoy!

1. Make bows and cut poinsettias from stems.

2. Attach bows to sides of floral plate.

3. Add poinsettias to base.

4. Add hydrangea blooms.

5. Insert berry picks.

6. Place candles on plate.

Designer's Tips

You can do floral centerpieces… I promise! Just take a deep breath, follow the directions and have fun. Step-by-step photographs are included to help you along.

You can customize your centerpiece by following a few guidelines:

Size
If you want to use a different type of flower than I've shown here, simply choose another flower that is about the same size. My main flower in this arrangement is the poinsettia. The hydrangea is the accent flower and the berries are filler. Just make sure that any florals you choose are about the same size and proportion.

Color
Colors should complement one another, not compete. One mistake beginners commonly make is to choose too many different colors. This arrangement features two basic colors, Burgundy poinsettias and berries and Ivory hydrangeas. The ribbon and candles also feature the same two colors. For best results, choose one main color and one accent color.

Christmas in the Woods

Dried fruit makes a naturally elegant accent in this candlescape. It's great for holiday or everyday decorating!

MATERIALS:
• 16" candle plate
• Two 6" tall and two 3" tall round pillars
• 2 ball candles
• Dried apple slices, orange slices and cinnamon sticks
INSTRUCTIONS:
Arrange candles on plate as desired. Surround with dried apple slices, cinnamon sticks and orange slices.

1. Arrange candles on the plate.

2. Place dried apples on plate.

3. Add the dried orange slices.

4. Place cinnamon sticks over dried fruit slices.

Orange & Eucalyptus

The colors of rich green and orange will make your table top glow.

MATERIALS:
- 6" pillar candle
- 7" brandy snifter
- 16" pre-made eucalyptus wreath
- Dried orange slices
- 9 artificial oranges
- Hot glue and glue sticks

INSTRUCTIONS:
Place brandy snifter in center of wreath and insert candle. Arrange oranges around wreath and glue to secure. Glue orange slices randomly on wreath.

Peppermint Pleasures

A fun, festive holiday project. Make a single arrangement, or group several together for a large centerpiece.

MATERIALS:
- Glass cylinder
- 12" wreath
- Red berries
- White berries
- Peppermint floating candle
- 3 yards of floral ribbon

INSTRUCTIONS:
Glue clusters of Red berries throughout the greenery branches. Accent with White berries. Attach a bow to the front of the arrangement. Place cylinder in center of wreath. Fill with water and float candle on top.

1. Glue clusters of berries in greenery.

2. Accent with White berries.

3. Attach bow to front.

4. Place cylinder in center, fill with water and add candle.

Blue Elegance

Dried woodland flowers, an elegant glass bowl and a deep blue candle bring a touch of natural wonder to any decor.

MATERIALS:
• 6" triple-wick candle
• 10" Clear glass bowl
• 16" pre-made dried flower wreath
INSTRUCTIONS:
Place bowl in center of wreath. Insert candle.

Mood Lighting

Set the mood with these softly glowing candle holders.

MATERIALS:
- 3 to 4 styles of exotic paper
- Plaid Royal Coat decoupage glue
- Foam brush
- Assorted glass candle holders

INSTRUCTIONS:

Tear or cut exotic papers into small pieces about 2" to 4". Apply Royal Coat to a 6" long portion of the candle holder. Place pieces of paper on the candle holder overlapping them so that no glass is left uncovered. Repeat until the entire candle holder is covered with paper. Apply a coat of decoupage glue over the paper and allow to dry. Trim any excess paper even with the top of the container. Place appropriate sized candles in the containers.

1. Tear paper into 2" to 4" pieces.

2. Apply Royal Coat.

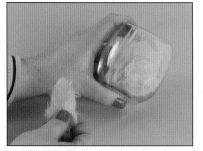

3. Place paper on holder overlapping edges.

4. Seal paper with Royal Coat.